Saved
But Not
Delivered

A Guide to Experience Joy and Peace

WANDA SCRUGGS ALLEN

Saved But Not Delivered: A Guide to Experience Joy and Peace

Copyright © 2019 Wanda Scruggs Allen

All rights reserved. Published in the United States.

Wanda@SavedButNotDelivered.com

This book contains Scripture verses from various versions of the Bible: New International Version ©2017, King James Version ©2017, American King James Version ©2017, New American Standard Bible ©2017, and the Modern English Version ©2017. Quotations from these sources are not a substantial contribution to the content of this book.

Library of Congress Cataloging-In-Publication Data

Scruggs Allen, Wanda

Saved but not delivered/Wanda Scruggs Allen

ISBN 978-0-9844475-7-2

1. Religious Warfare   2. Religions & Inspirations

Library of Congress Control Number: 2017949372

Cover design by Stacey Grainger

Interior design by Stacey Grainer

Printed in the United States of America

First Edition

To My Parents
Pastor Walter W. Scruggs and the Late Anna M. Scruggs
Memorial Gospel Crusades Church
Philadelphia, Pennsylvania

TABLE OF CONTENTS

	Foreword	vi
	Introduction	ix
Chapter 1	Jonah…Not Delivered!	1
Chapter 2	Salvation vs. Deliverance	9
Chapter 3	Disagreeing With God	17
Chapter 4	Salvation Revisited	27
Chapter 5	Seven Steps to Deliverance	37
Chapter 6	Understanding God's Love	51
Chapter 7	Press On…Don't Look Back!	59
	References	67
	About the Author	68

FOREWORD

Peace is experienced through an inner contentment threaded in the confidence of our Savior.

> *"Peace. It does not mean to be in a place where there is no noise, trouble or hard work. It means to be in the midst of those things and still be calm in your heart."*
>
> (author unknown)

Saved by the blood of Jesus Christ, we have an awesome opportunity to be delivered into the hands of both peace and joy. How we choose to experience the love of God determines the manifestation of wholeness and wellness for each of us. Allen reminds each of us that joy is expressed in the pleasure and state of satisfaction. While death is in the bowels of the disobedient, life swells the veins of those who are obedient to God's will, commandments, and plans. Obedience crafts a cradle of confidence wherein the promises of God are awakened. In this way, awakening renders deliverance and deliverance is about freedom. Through deliverance, we are free from eternal condemnation and liberated to experience everlasting life.

Knowing who we are listening to is important, however, understanding who we are hearing from is critical. As you interact with the pages of *Saved…But Not Delivered*, my hope is that you experience freedom in ways that passes all human comprehension.

This freedom allows you to deny self and joyfully serve others. It compels you to love others as Christ loved the church. This kind of freedom opens the floodgates of faith that slays doubt, fear, and uncertainty. In God's deliverance, we are postured to cleverly operate in the gifts bestowed upon us, overshadowed by the mercy and love of our Father.

Love, peace, and joy!

Larthenia Howard, EdD, CPP
Award Winning Author and Publisher
WriteABookIn31Days.com

INTRODUCTION

I am truly amazed whenever I discover how unhappy some Christians are and the trouble that they cause because of it. Of course, we go through periods of grief resulting from a lost, a disappointment or a tragic event. Life brings deep emotional wounds for many of us in both expected and unexpected ways. However, we are declared a victorious people, born to a Father who has everlasting love, grace, and mercy. Tapping into this truth is the lifeline of humanity.

The Bible assures us that Jesus is the great physician, counselor and Savior. He has a plan for everyone if we can just get into agreement with God. We can be not only saved but delivered from thoughts and experiences that provoke so much unhappiness.

Like Jonah, there are some believers who are simply unhappy because they have never allowed God to come into every room of their heart and change their perspective. And still, there are others who have never been delivered from their debilitating mindset. They really want to dictate to God the plan for their life, family and ministry as if they know more.

Oftentimes as in the life of Jonah, God literally makes you complete His will and plan that should bring joy. Although this sentiment is not always experienced. To experience the kind of unspeakable joy we sing about, you must be renewed by God's transforming power.

God is a God of Love! He shows us in the Book of Jonah that much unhappiness comes because we simply don't agree with His plan. God sent Jonah to a wicked nation to preach repentance so that the people could be reconciled to Him. However, Jonah disagreed and wanted them killed. The results of disagreeing with God and His Word can lead to sin, insecurity, jealousy, unhappiness and condemnation that places blame on others.

It is my sincere hope that the body of Christ, the church, will answer the call of God and come into agreement with His plan to be saved and delivered. In this way, we can experience real joy and peace and be effective in letting our light shine for Christ Jesus who has a wonderful plan for everyone.

Saved…But Not Delivered: A Guide to Experience Joy and Peace can be used as a resource for tapping in to life's greatest reward…a life of unspeakable joy, peace, and love. As you are reminded, or perhaps introduced to God's grace and love, it is my deepest hope that you are open to hear the spirit of the Lord speak to you personally. Truthfully engage in the reflection questions at the end of each chapter and anticipate and experience of joy and peace everlasting.

Chapter 1

Jonah...
Not Delivered

Saved But Not Delivered: A Guide to Experience Joy and Peace

Jonah 3:1-2 (AKJV)

"And the word of the Lord came unto Jonah the second time, saying, Arise, go unto Nineveh, that great city and preach unto it the preaching that I bid thee."

In the Holy Bible there is a story about a man named Jonah. Jonah was a very talented and skillful individual who God used as his mouthpiece, a prophet. Jonah lived centuries before the birth of Christ and he functioned as an evangelist does today traveling, preaching, and reconciling mankind to God. Jonah had a relationship with God wherein he understood God's character and love for mankind. However, Jonah did not share that same love for all mankind nor did he allow God to change his mind.

In the Book of Jonah, God gave specific instructions to preach to the wicked. Jonah was directed to travel to Nineveh for this mission. Instead of obeying God, Jonah boarded a ship and went to Tarshish, a completely opposite direction. Shortly afterwards, a storm arose. Jonah shared with the men on the boat that he was the reason for the storm and requested that they throw him overboard into the raging sea. Though the men did not want to cast him overboard, they had no choice but to obey the prophet of God. Jonah was cast into the sea and immediately the waters calmed. Forever vigilant with a plan for Jonah's life, God prepared a great fish to swallow him. While in the belly of the fish for three days, Jonah repented of his disobedience and the great fish spat him on dry ground.

The commandment to go to Nineveh came to Jonah a second time. This time Jonah obeyed. He led an entire nation to repentance and God spared the people. However, Jonah was furious with God for not destroying the people. He had a different opinion about the matter and wanted to run the ministry his way. In the Book of Romans 12:2 (AKJV) it states, *"And be not conformed to this world: but be ye transformed by the renewing of your mind, that ye may prove what is that good, and acceptable, and perfect, will of God."* Jonah's mind was never renewed to see people as God saw them, worthy to be saved. It was the will of God to save the people of Nineveh but it was Jonah's will to see them killed. Though Jonah had the ability to lead multitudes to the Lord, his thinking and his actions were rebellious.

We read in Jonah 4:2 that Jonah had full knowledge of God's grace, mercy, and kindness - and of his slowness to anger. This is why Jonah did not want to go to the city of Nineveh. However, Jonah was created and gifted by God to fulfill God's purpose. God had given Jonah the understanding of his abilities and skills to lead people to Him.

In several ways, Jonah was symbolic of Jesus Christ. He was sent to a nation with a mission to lead the people to repentance and reconciliation to God. Jonah spent three days in the belly of a fish and rose in a miraculous way, much like Christ rose from the dead on the third day. Too, Jonah was sent to the Gentiles, just as Jesus Christ solidified salvation for all after resurrection and the ascension.

At the same time, Jonah also typified man's struggles with the flesh. Much like Jonah, God sends us to do a work for Him even though we are not completely delivered of our own opinion concerning God's work. God does not wait for us to be completely delivered…even in our minds. Many of us are healed along the way as the lepers who were healed by Christ Jesus as they moved forward in faith. In the Book of John, chapter 17, is a story of Jesus healing the ten lepers. As the ten lepers obeyed Jesus and went forward to show themselves to the priest, they were healed. The healing takes place as the leapers went…not before they went. This tells us that as we move forward in faith, God will move on our behalf as well.

It is God's hope that as we go forward, we grow and begin to show the world God's love, grace, mercy and kindness. It is also God's hope that our minds be renewed daily and we see situations the way He sees them. He longs for us to love people enough to lead them to Christ Jesus.

Some Christians have no joy and peace because they just don't like God's agenda. God saves, forgives and raises up whom he wants to use. Unfortunately, there are some Christians who are angry, like Jonah, about God's love, grace, mercy, kindness and slowness to anger. Some preachers avoid preaching about grace and mercy. Some leaders in the church don't speak about God's grace and mercy. The sadness is that when we do the will of God with the wrong perception or deny the truth of God's love, we can become angry with God, much like Jonah expressed.

As God leads us, we need to examine ourselves to make sure we have the mind of God. In 2nd Corinthians 13:5 (AKJV), the Word of God states, *"Examine yourselves, whether ye be in the faith...."* This means that we need to check ourselves to see if we are thinking and moving with God. If not, the enemy will use our flesh for his agenda. In Jonah 4:3 (AKJV), Jonah became depressed and had a desire to quit and die. Jonah said, *"Therefore now, O Lord, take, I beseech thee, my life from me; for it is better for me to die than to live."* Jonah's refusal to yield to God's complete will made him an unhappy believer.

The root problem was Jonah's refusal to agree with God. His disagreement led to sin and all the consequences of unrepentant sin. Similar consequences happen today. There are unhappy believers because like Jonah, they disagree with God. They are not willing to yield their opinions and their will to a loving omniscient God. In other words, though they received the gift of salvation, they have not yielded their thoughts and opinions to agree with God. They haven't allowed God to deliver them from themselves. They are saved, but not delivered.

REFLECTIONS

What are or were your disagreements with God's Word? What are your perceptions of God's Word? Do your perceptions align with what the Word says?

REFLECTIONS

In what way(s) have you surrendered to God's Word? If you haven't surrendered, what continues to be your struggle in trusting God?

Saved But Not Delivered: A Guide to Experience Joy and Peace

CHAPTER 2

Salvation vs. Deliverance

Saved But Not Delivered: A Guide to Experience Joy and Peace

James 4:1 (AKJV)

"What causes fights and quarrels among you? Don't they come from your desires that battle within you?"

One Sunday after morning worship, a mother of our church who has gone to be with the Lord, walked up to me and said, "Wanda, everybody is not delivered." She said this is an attempt to encourage me after observing a disrespectful interaction. Instantly, I knew what she meant. Some people are believers in Christ but have not allowed God to transform them from their destructive behavior to one more Christ-like. I was a young woman when she said this and still today, I reflect on this statement whenever I encounter Christians behaving unseemly. Her wisdom reminds me to forgive and continue to move forward.

It was the "spiritual wickedness in high places" mentioned in the book of Ephesians that wanted to discourage me as I worked with the youth and music ministry in the church. Ephesians 6:11-12 (AKJV) states, *"Put on the whole armor of God, that ye may be able to stand against the wiles of the devil. For we wrestle not against flesh and blood, but against principalities, against powers, against the rulers of the darkness of this world, against spiritual wickedness in high places."* Mother Hayes understood this and didn't just sit on the sidelines to watch the battle; she got involved and did as the Scriptures said in Titus chapter two…teach the younger women. I soon realized that those who launched attacks, those who stood by and watched the battle, and those who did or said nothing, were one and the same, ***not delivered.***

Some people can watch a hard-working person under attack and not intervene with a kind word, or prayer to stop an attack, even if they possess the power or influence for a counteraction. Unfortunately, this happens because they have areas in their life in which they are not delivered from as well. They may secretly enjoy the bullying and the slandering, hoping for that person to be moved out of position even though it is the place God has put the accused person for His purpose.

Christ Jesus came, died and rose again for the saving of souls. Every attack is inspired by our enemy, Satan. His goal is for souls to be scattered or unreachable. Christians who refuse to allow God to "deliver" them from ungodly perceptions and ways will ignorantly follow the wickedness that is whispered into their ears. The Bible explains fighting among us in the book of James. James 4:1-3 (NIV) states, *"What causes fight and quarrels among you? Don't they come from your desires that battle within you? You desire but do not have, so you kill. You covet but you cannot get what you want, so you quarrel and fight. You do not have because you do not ask God. When you ask, you do not receive, because you ask with wrong motives, that you may spend what you get on your pleasures."* I soon realized that every attack on me wasn't totally about me at all. There was a spiritual war happening to shut down ministries and destroy lives.

Christians who have accepted the gift of salvation but unwilling to transform, are ineffective or limited in the very thing in which they want to be successful. This is a result of their refusal to let go and let God have his way. Some are real troublemakers in the church and in their families. They haven't allowed God to deliver them from their issues and way of thinking, therefore they do not transition with God. As God is trying to transform them, they fight and blame others for their discomfort.

If we are really honest with ourselves and in touch with God, we will acknowledge that we all are in transition. God is forever moving and so are we. In the Book of James 4:14 (AKJV) it says, *"...For what is your life? It is even a vapour that appeareth for a little time, and then vanisheth away."* Since we are all transitioning, it would be wise to transition with God. It is impossible to stay the same. In our efforts to be in control, we become stagnant. Anything that is stagnant, such as water, becomes impure and not fit for drinking or washing. By not listening to the Holy Spirit we become stagnant and naturally move backward.

There are Christians who don't smoke, drink, commit adultery or fornication and believe that they are living in obedience and pleasing God. Though a disciplined life has its rewards, it is not necessarily a life pleasing to God. This would make God very shallow and only observant of outward appearances. After receiving the gift of salvation, the only way that we can truly please God and experience real joy and peace is to allow

Him to renew our minds. Short of this revelation, we will end up like Jonah, the great prophet of God in the Old Testament who was talented, miserable, and mean.

I've have had several unpleasant experiences with spiteful people in the church. Though they caused me problems, the effects on their children were worse. I refer to their offspring as the children born in the wilderness. In the book of Exodus, many children were born in the wilderness when they should have been born in the Promise Land. The journey through the wilderness should have taken 40 days but because of disobedience it took 40 years. As a result, children were born into a wilderness experience. It was my experience that even though the children were brought to church, they lived in a home with disobedient and undelivered parents who caused them to miss out on many Godly experiences. In fact, they missed God completely, bringing shame on their parents. What makes matters worse is that these were the parents, like Pharisees, that were so proud of their holy living. You wouldn't find them sitting in a bar or involved in an illicit relationship. But you could find them in activities and conversations that would hinder the ministry. Like Jonah, they had their picks on whom God should call and whom He should not.

Fortunately for us, God doesn't ask for anyone's opinion when it comes to who He will bless or raise up to expand His territory. This was Jonah's problem. He wanted to run the ministry his way and was angry. Without God's transforming power, we can be a modern day Jonah, ***saved but not delivered.***

REFLECTIONS

"that if you confess with your mouth Jesus is Lord, and believe in your heart that God has raised Him from the dead, you will be saved; for with the heart one believes unto righteousness, and with the mouth confession is made unto salvation."

Romans 10:9-10 (MEV)

Reflecting on the scripture above, have you accepted the gift of salvation? Why or why not? If so, what is your testimony? If not, what is your reason for not accepting this wonderful gift, or what is it that you do not understand?

Wanda Scruggs Allen

REFLECTIONS

What experiences have helped shape your opinion of God in a positive or negative way? Has this impacted your belief or disbelief in God?

CHAPTER 3

Disagreeing With God

Saved But Not Delivered: A Guide to Experience Joy and Peace

Jonah 1:3 (AKJV)

"But Jonah rose up to flee unto Tarshish from the presence of the Lord......."

There is much that we can learn by examining the scriptures and Jonah's refusal to agree with God that ultimately led him to a life of misery. There are several consequences of not having your mind renewed by God. We will explore several of them by considering the life and actions of Jonah. Through this examination, we can avoid becoming a modern-day Jonah and accept the mind and will of God that leads to a life of joy and peace. But first, let's review the consequences of Jonah's disagreement with God and what can translate as modern-day consequences if we refuse to agree with God.

- **Move in the wrong direction.** Jonah's disagreement with God led to disobedience and caused him to move in the opposite direction. He was openly defiant and found himself in the belly of a great fish. When we obey our flesh and not the leading of the Holy Spirit, we move contrary to the way God moves. If you're in a leadership role, you may blame people for lack of support and abandonment, when in fact, you may not be in sync with God. Doing what you want to do inevitably results in failure.

- **Place others in jeopardy.** Everyone connected to Jonah's disobedience suffered with him aboard the ship. A storm came to alarm the crew. They had to obey the Prophet Jonah and throw him overboard so they could be saved. Jonah's disobedience placed others in a life and death situation. This tells us that those who depend and look to us for support and leadership are in trouble if we don't have a renewed mind to obey God. In the home, children will suffer calamities and learn ungodly ways to address life's difficulties. They simply will not believe in God. Disobedience opens doors for Satan to infiltrate his plan to steal, kill and destroy.

- **Wasted time.** Time is precious and costly. Jonah's decision to disobey God caused him to be in a messy situation, the nasty belly of a great fish. Opportunities can be lost through wasted time. It is dangerous to be in the wrong place at the wrong time.

- **Disobedience in ministry.** God wanted to save the people of Nineveh. However, Jonah wanted to go and preach to people of his own choosing. Jonah wanted to run the ministry his way and not God's way. If our minds are not constantly renewed by God, we can think the church and/or ministry should revolve around us because of the position we occupy. The ministry must be Christ-centered, a reflection of God's love for mankind. Jesus Christ came for the needs of people. The needs of the people come first, not what we want to see happen. When we put God first in our lives, then we will put the needs of the people first. God always leads for the body of Christ to be edified.

- **Lost desire to live - depression and bitterness.** Jonah's un-renewed mind led him to be depressed, bitter and with no desire to live. Jonah stated in 4:3(NIV), *"Now, Lord, take away my life, for it is better for me to die than to live."* When our thoughts and actions are out of the will of God, it will lead to misery. It is so important to view life through the eyes of God. We must see and value people the way God sees and values them. After all, Christ Jesus felt that mankind was worth dying for in order to redeem. He went to the cross for our sins and rose so that we can rise above any situation, even death.

- **Refuse to see God bless others.** Because God forgave the people, Jonah fled. In Jonah chapter 4, we see how angry he was because God forgave the people when they repented and turned from their wickedness. In verse 5, we see that he could not stay but left the city of Nineveh and made a booth for himself so he could see what would happen to the city. When we don't understand God's purpose for salvation and blessings for all mankind, we can become angry and refuse to rejoice when people are blest. Jonah had no joy. In fact, he refused to remain when the blessings of God poured out upon the repented nation. When God pours out blessings upon those who have surrendered their life to Christ Jesus, Christians today can refuse to celebrate as well. Jonah's un-renewed mind missed the entire purpose and plan of God.

- **Wrong motives for preaching and teaching.** Jonah wanted the people condemned and not saved. He wanted "an eye for an eye" and "a tooth for a tooth." Jonah wanted revenge. His love for mankind was not like God's. When our minds are not renewed to God's perspective, our flesh and natural desires reign instead of the will of God. We do things with the wrong intentions, hoping that things will work out on its own. Because God is ultimately in control, circumstances will work for the good. This happens on God's terms and often cause displeasure for the one who has disagreed with God and refused to repent.

- **Perception and discernment impeded.** Jonah felt pity for the plant (gourd) that provided shade for him and died (Jonah4:9). Ironically, Jonah did not feel any pity for a nation of 120 thousand. His discernment was completely distorted. Jonah no longer knew what was important.

- It is vital that we transition with God or we lose touch with reality and what is important. Many times people think that they can skip the process of being transformed, remain in disagreement with God, and still complete God's will with joy. But in reality, disagreement with God and skipping the transformation process of seeing situations through the eyes of God will revoke discernment that is needed for "next steps." After Jonah finally completed the will of God and was angry about the peoples' salvation, he moved further into oblivion. He could not comprehend the next step so he ended up sitting on a hill, complaining to God about not killing them. God attempted to comfort him from the hot sun. There was a breeze from a east wind and a gourd that miraculously grew in one night. When the plant was eaten by a worm and died, Jonah's discernment caused him to feel pity for the plant, rather than the wicked people who God saved. Yet, the Lord continued to communicate with Jonah in an attempt to win him over. Nevertheless, the Bible never mentioned Jonah's agreement with God, nor his experience of pleasure with the sparing of Nineveh.

- **Miss God's love for mankind.** Before God came to the earth in the form of a man, Christ Jesus, God sent Jonah to preach repentance so that the people would not be lost and separated from God eternally. Jonah is a type of Christ. However, Jonah did not have the mind or the love of God for mankind. He had no joy in God saving the people from destruction. He wished the opposite. He was completely miserable, as so many Christians are today who have not yielded their opinion to God. Miserable Christians can always trace their unhappiness back to some disagreement with God. John 3:16 (AKJV) says, *"For God so loved the world that He sent his only begotten Son that whosoever believeth on Him should not perish but have ever lasting life."* This scripture is about Christ Jesus being the sacrificial lamb of God. God loves people so much that He made a way through his Son Jesus for us to be reconciled unto Him. Because of the Christ's shed blood, we have the victory over every binding thing.

- **Limitations instead of expectations.** We can learn from Jonah that when we do not agree with God, we limit ourselves. We stunt our growth personally. Though Jonah was forced to do what God told him to do, his heart was far from the purpose and plan of God. We never heard of any other great revivals that he did. In fact, that one revival of leading a whole nation of 120 thousand to God and being miserable because of it, is all that we know about that great and talented prophet named Jonah.

However, we can live with great expectation of God's promises. Jeremiah 29:11(NIV) says, *"For I know the plans I have for you," declares the Lord, plans to prosper you and not to harm you, plans to give you hope and a future."* We can live with joy and peace if we can just agree with God's plan for our life.

There is no peace or victory in disagreeing with an intelligent, all knowing God. It is disheartening to see people formulate their own opinion only to miss out on the blessings that they so desperately want and need. God is a loving God who wants to bless and not punish. He paid it all on the cross so that we may live victoriously.

REFLECTIONS

What consequences, if any, have you experienced from not agreeing with God? How did you resolve it?

REFLECTIONS

How did you emotionally feel when you disagreed or agreed with God?

Chapter 4

Salvation Revisited

Saved But Not Delivered: A Guide to Experience Joy and Peace

Revelation 3:20 (NASB)

Behold, I stand at the door and knock. If anyone hears My voice and opens the door, I will come in to him and dine with him, and he with Me.

Jonah was symbolic of Jesus Christ coming to a world that needed to be reconciled to God. He preached the word of God and a nation repented and escaped damnation. Salvation is immediate when we accept the wonderful gift that God has for us. Jesus is knocking on the door of our heart and the only thing that we have to do is open up our heart's door. Salvation is simple and not complicated. That's why it is easy for children to understand and believe.

Adults can make salvation a bitter pill to swallow. I can remember being ill as a child and gaging on aspirin to make me well. In some circles, that is how salvation is introduced. People are told of a list of things that they must give up in order to be saved and they cannot comprehend living without "The List." Some things on the list were cultural and robbed people of the very talents that God blessed them with, such as acting and dancing. However, whatever is on the so-called list that will hinder our growth, God will reveal after salvation as our mind is renewed daily. We must share the good news of Jesus Christ. Salvation is not about a list of things that we must give up or delete. It is receiving what God has done and accepting Him as Lord and Savior. We learn from Romans 2:4 that it is the goodness of God that leads us to repent and transform.

In Ephesians 2:8 (AKJV), the gift of salvation is explained. *"For by grace are ye saved through faith; and that not of yourselves: it is the gift of God."* Salvation has been taught erroneously as a list of things that you must give up, making a life with Christ seem difficult, boring, uneventful and not prosperous. However, Christ Jesus is a giver and not a taker. A relationship with God through Jesus Christ enhances your life and gives purpose and meaning. In fact, Christ comes in and defines everything that you were given at birth. Christ Jesus sharpens every skill and talent. It is difficult to write with a dull pencil point. It is the sharpening and the shaving of the pencil that produce a point for writing that makes it effective. And so it is with salvation. After we received the gift, the Holy Spirit does the sharpening and shaving as we agree with God and allow Him to lead us.

A minister shared his testimony of the day he accepted Jesus Christ as his Lord and Savior. He went to church infrequently because of his wife's request and daughter who sang in the youth choir. At this time in his life, he was only there to support his daughter. One day he walked down the aisle of the church and gave his heart to God. After attending Sunday morning services, bible classes and prayer meetings, he said the Holy Spirit led him to give up ownership of the two well established bars in the community. This happened months after salvation occurred in his life. I love his testimony because many still don't believe that after we received the gift of salvation, we need room and time to grow to be what God has called us to be.

Even in my own life, I didn't accept the gift of salvation because I thought salvation was linked to my attire, (not wearing pants), not dancing, and a list of don'ts. My perception of God was gloom and doom. Condemnation was so commonplace that I believed it drove my generation away from the body of Christ. I thought God was a taker and not a giver. There were so many rules linked to salvation and/or disobedience. The condemnation varied from church to church and crossed denominations.

At the age of 21, I decided to truly follow Jesus and realized that the rules were bondage and nothing more than the church culture and/or condemnation. There was much emphasis placed on outward appearance and all of the don'ts. Those with issues of control and who needed deliverance were quite comfortable and quite mean. I didn't waste any time ignoring the pressure to look a certain way or to be quiet because I was a woman. Still, some felt it was their duty to encourage me to not wear make-up, pants, tailored suits, and my favorite red dress that almost hit my ankles. I ignored it all because I had truly been discipled. I had the joy of the Lord living on the inside and wasn't going to let anyone put me in bondage or deceive me about the love of God and his Holy Spirit that dwelled within me. Today, many of those people are all wearing make-up, pants, and making their own fashion statements while serving God. Unlike Jonah, they transformed and grew in the Lord.

Discipleship takes time, especially if you've been taught erroneously. I am pleased to share that my greatest experience with God is when he knocked on the door of my heart and I let Him in to validate my existence with His love and grace. And when you are validated by God and receive the love He has for you, you can stand tall and walk away from any foolishness that may come your way!

When we receive the gift of salvation, our spirit is saved, not our soul or our body. We are spirit, soul, and body. This is explained in I Thessalonians 5:23 (AKJV), *"... I pray God your whole spirit and soul and body be preserved blameless unto the coming of our Lord Jesus Christ."* We open the door of our heart and Jesus comes in and gives us His Holy Spirit to dwell inside of us and thus we are saved! Our spirit is saved and we have the indwelling of the Holy Spirit. The soul is our "mind and will." After our spirit is saved, we now have God's power for our minds to be renewed and to bring our bodies into the will of God. We have to agree with God for our minds to be renewed and for our bodies to submit to the will of God. The Bible encourages us to cast down thoughts and lifestyles that are contrary to God's will. It states in 2 Corinthians 10:5 (AKJV), *"Casting down imaginations, and every high thing that exalteth itself against the knowledge of God, and bringing into captivity every thought to the obedience of Christ."* Figuratively speaking, we allow Jesus to come into every room of our house and give Him permission to redesign it. In return, He will dine with us, feed us, and give us a purpose and successful plan for our life. That's why Jesus said in Revelations 3:20(NASB), *"Behold, I stand at the door and knock. If anyone hears My voice and opens the door, I will come in to him and dine with him, and he with Me."*

Saved But Not Delivered: A Guide to Experience Joy and Peace

In the book of Matthew chapter 25, Jesus compared the kingdom of heaven to a man who gave his three servants talents. Two of the servants doubled what was given to them and one servant buried his talent and did nothing with what was given to him. Jesus called the servant who buried his talent and did nothing, an "unprofitable servant." It is God's expectation for believers to use what He has given them, be blessed, and be a blessing to others. Salvation comes with great rewards and blessings if we have the faith to truly follow Christ Jesus.

We receive the Lord Jesus Christ into our lives by believing with our heart and confessing with our mouth. Romans 10:9,10 (NIV) states, *"...If you declare with your mouth, "Jesus is Lord," and believe in your heart that God raised him from the dead, you will be saved. For it is with your heart that you believe and are justified, and it is with your mouth that you profess your faith and are saved."* Salvation is the beginning of our walk with God through believing and confessing the Lord Jesus Christ. A model prayer for salvation can be the following:

> *"Dear God, I hear you calling me to be one of your children. I believe that you sent your son Jesus to live, die and rise again just for me. Please come into my heart as my Lord and Savior and forgive me of all of my sins. I ask you this with thanksgiving for the wonderful gift of salvation! Amen!"*

Again, through salvation comes the gift of the Holy Spirit who lives inside of us to comfort and lead. Our spirit is made anew and we have the indwelling of the Holy Spirit. We are no longer alone and we are able to talk and walk with God daily. After salvation several things such as deliverance, healing, purpose and direction can come. However, we must agree with God to bring our soul *(mind and will),* and our body into subjection to experience joy and peace. We cannot be victorious if we are bitter like Jonah.

REFLECTIONS

I Thessalonians 5:23, (AKJV)

"... I pray God your whole spirit and soul and body be preserved blameless unto the coming of our Lord Jesus Christ."

Reflect on Chapter 4 and the above scripture. What does this scripture mean to you? What can you do to be without blame when you stand before the Lord Jesus Christ?

Wanda Scruggs Allen

REFLECTIONS

Corinthians 10:5 (AKJV)

"Casting down imaginations, and every high thing that exalteth itself against the knowledge of God, and bringing into captivity every thought to the obedience of Christ."

Reflect on Chapter 4 and the above scripture. What is the Holy Spirit communicating to you personally? What are some of your past and present thoughts or situations that must come into the obedience of God's word?

_____

_____

_____

_____

_____

_____

_____

_____

_____

Chapter 5

Seven Steps to Deliverance

Saved But Not Delivered: A Guide to Experience Joy and Peace

Romans 12:2(AKJV)

"And be not conformed to this world: but be ye transformed by the renewing of your mind, that ye may prove what is that good, and acceptable, and perfect, will of God."

When we think of the word deliverance, images of being rescued may come to mind. I view deliverance as allowing God to transform us by the renewing of our minds and revealing what is in our heart so that we may know what is the good, acceptable and the perfect will of God. This is truly deliverance because our minds and heart are bound with fear, foolishness and other things that have been brought about by the spiritual wickedness in high places as mentioned in the book of Ephesians. Ephesians 6: 10-13 (AKJV) states, *"Finally, my brethren, be strong in the Lord, and in the power of his might. Put on the whole armour of God that ye may be able to stand against the wiles of the devil. For we wrestle not against flesh and blood, but against principalities, against powers, against the rulers of the darkness of this world, against spiritual wickedness in high places. Wherefore take unto you the whole armour of God that ye may be able to withstand in the evil day, and having done all, to stand."*

In addition, the Bible tells us in 2 Timothy 1:7 (AKJV), *"God has not given us the spirit of fear but of power, love and a sound mind."* The NIV translation states, *"For the Spirit God gave us does not make us timid, but gives us power, love and self-discipline."* Therefore, we need to be delivered from every imagination and fear that exalted itself higher than the Word of God. This is reiterated in 2 Corinthians 10:5, *"Casting down imaginations, and every high thing that exalteth itself against the knowledge of God, and bringing into captivity every thought to the obedience of Christ."* This means that our mind and heart need to be delivered before we can really obey God. Our opinion has to be replaced with God's viewpoint. The NIV translation states, *"We demolish arguments and every pretension that sets itself up against the knowledge of God, and we take captive every thought to make it obedient to Christ."*

Salvation came with the gift of the Holy Spirit living on the inside of you. Because of this, we have the power to choose God's will and way and serve Him with joy and peace. Salvation gave us the power to live victoriously, rather than a slave to sin. As we go through the process of allowing God to change our minds, He will reveal what is in our hearts, the core of our joy and pain. Positive thinking alone does not change us.

Below are 7 steps that will lead you to deliverance and a life of joy and peace.

Step 1: Accept the Gift of Salvation

Romans 10:9, 10 (NIV) states, "..If you declare with your mouth, "Jesus is Lord," and believe in your heart that God raised him from the dead, you will be saved. For it is with your heart that you believe and are justified, and it is with your mouth that you profess your faith and are saved."

Salvation is the beginning of our walk with God. Positive thinking alone cannot bring the deliverance and peace that we need. We need a relationship with the one and only loving God. Through salvation, we have the power to say no to demonic plans and say yes to God's plan for our life. Salvation places us in right standing with God by moving us into the family of God. Again, you can say the following prayer below!

"Dear God, I hear you calling me to be one of your children. I believe that you sent your son Jesus to live, die and rise again just for me. Please come into my heart as my Lord and Savior and forgive me of all of my sins. I ask you this with thanksgiving for the wonderful gift of salvation! Amen!"

Jesus said He is knocking on our heart's door.

Revelations 3:20 (NASB) reminds us, *"Behold, I stand at the door and knock. If anyone hears My voice and opens the door, I will come in to him and dine with him, and he with Me."* God is waiting for us to accept the wonderful gift of salvation.

Step 2: Agree with what God says about Himself, you, and others.

John 3:17 (AKJV) reveals, *"For God did not send His Son into the world to condemn the world, but that the world through Him might be saved."* Many see God as one who came to punish mankind. But Jesus said He came not to condemn people but to save them. We see in the gospel of Matthew and Mark that Jesus was moved with compassion. He healed, saved, taught and performed many miracles. Matthew 14:14 (AKJV) states, *"And Jesus went forth, and saw a great multitude, and was moved with compassion toward them, and he healed their sick."* And still we see His work here, *"And Jesus, when he came out, saw much people, and was moved with compassion toward them, because they were as sheep not having a shepherd: and he began to teach them many things"* (Mark 6:34, AKJV). Jesus led by example and showed why He came to earth…to save, heal, and deliver. We must agree on God's purpose for mankind.

Psalms 139:14 (AKJV) shares, *"I will praise thee; for I am fearfully and wonderfully made: marvelous are thy works; and that my soul knoweth right well."* This scripture says that we must agree with what God says about us regardless of how we have been treated. As a minister, I have prayed and ministered to many that still suffer from low self-esteem started as a child in the home. I am glad that physical and sexual abuse of children has finally come to the forefront and people can receive the help they need. But there is still a very subtle thing that happens to the young in the home that screams, "I don't love you or you're not worthy of all of my love." I know of a youth who protested about how badly she was treated in the family. The oldest sibling justified it by stating, "In every family there is one child who gets no respect and is picked upon and in this family, it is you!"

These negative experiences of not being validated plague our families and are very powerful in destroying lives. Black sheep are created within the family dynamics and some face lifelong struggles because of it. Sadly, Satan sows seeds of destruction early in life and many of it comes from the very people that should have come with encouragement.

Nevertheless, just as Joseph, in the book of Genesis, was thrown into a pit by his brothers to be killed, many have been thrown into pits by family members, family friends, or church family. But God always has a plan for everyone to go from the pit to the palace if we follow Him. Many of us have our stories to tell of how the devil tried to destroy us. He never stops. But God in His infinite mercy and grace has worked it all out for the good. If we agree with what God is saying about us, we can receive His love and the validation that we need. We will become more sensitive and confident in doing God's will. God will consistently deliver us as we listen to His voice. It is not a one-time event.

Jesus said in John 13:34-35 (AKJV), "A new commandment I give unto you, That ye love one another; as I have loved you, that ye also love one another. By this shall all men know that ye are my disciples, if ye have love one to another." Jesus gave this commandment that we must love one another. Our distinction in this world must be of love.

When I was in college, I went to hear a popular speaker. I went to be inspired as many of my college peers. Instead, the speech was mainly about the hatred Blacks should have for the White man and the White Jesus that many African Americans were following. The hatred spurred by the speaker was disturbing. He was brutal! And though I was not committed to following Jesus Christ at the time, I knew that I wasn't going to follow Him or any God that the speaker represented. In fact, I was afraid of a riot breaking out and not getting safely back to the dormitory. He created an atmosphere of hate and uncertainty.

Even in the church, it is not unusual, to find hater talk about members in the congregation. I have witnessed pleasant and supportive parishioners turn awry after seated around someone's dining room table engaged in negative talk. After they change company, they apologize for their behavior and become supportive again. I've witnessed several people warp the minds of adults and teenagers through character assassination. We must agree that God truly loves all people and does not want us to assassinate each other and destroy ministries. We must agree to love one another.

Step 3: Agree to be transformed by the renewing of your mind.

God delivers us daily by the renewing of our minds. The Bible states in Romans 12:1-2 (AKJV), *"I beseech you therefore, brethren, by the mercies of God, that ye present your bodies a living sacrifice, holy, acceptable unto God, which is your reasonable service. And be not conformed to this world: but be ye transformed by the renewing of your mind, that ye may prove what is that good, and acceptable, and perfect, will of God."* We are encouraged that we will be transformed if we allow God to transform our minds. One of my childhood Sunday school songs had lyrics that read, "I will make you fishers of men." The second verse of that song was, "Read your Bible, pray every day and you'll grow, grow, grow." As I discovered, when you read your Bible and pray every day, God will show you, YOU. God will show you areas of your life that you must yield to Him if you want to be prosperous and effective. Though we are "Saved," we still must choose God's perspective and His way of doing things. Yet many of us hold on to our way of thinking and operating and are defeated. Therefore, we miss personal blessings and a chance to be a blessing to others.

As I mentioned earlier, at the age of 21, the Lord drew me to Him and I committed my life to the Lord Jesus Christ. I allowed Christ to transform me by the renewing of my mind and the satanic effects of low self-esteem dissipated. I allowed Christ to define me, validate me, and then I walked in victory. I became focused and content as I walked and obeyed God.

Satan was so angry that he tried hard to destroy my confidence that came from a relationship with Christ Jesus. When I was unsaved, confused, and made mistakes, there were people in my life who didn't seem to be bothered at all. But when I got a clue to who I was in Christ Jesus and let God define me, OMG... the demons came out to get me. Still today, I pray for the intentions of how wicked people can be when you're not making a mess out of your life. Because God has transformed me, I believe He can transform anyone. So, I have to keep praying for souls to be saved, healed, and delivered. It's disturbing to see the consequences of unrepentant sin. However, the beauty of following Jesus Christ is that He will make you to be strong, resilient, and sensitive to minister.

Step 4: Know that God has a plan for your life.

In Jeremiah 29:11 we find, *"For I know the plans that I have for you, says the Lord, plans for peace and not for evil, to give you a future and a hope (MEV)."* Knowing that God has a plan for your life is a motivator within itself. I am often told by those who were raised in the church that they had no idea that God had a plan just for them. In many churches, the culture taught that the work of the church came first. Therefore, many children and adults missed opportunities to be developed.

The real ministry of the church is the *"salvation and development"* of its people, discipleship. The people are *"the church"* that God is coming back for; wherein, the *"needs of the people"* is the ministry. When this premise is not properly taught or executed, people have no idea that God has a plan for their life and find church attendance irrelevant to what is happening in their lives and in the real world. In other words, discipleship before church work is key. Jesus Christ said in John 10:10 (MEV), *"The thief does not come, except to steal and kill and destroy. I came that they may have life, and that they may have it more abundantly."* Jesus came to give a life plan for each and every one.

The church culture can rob you of this understanding by placing "church work" before the emotional, physical and spiritual needs of the people to be developed. It is crucial that the church makes disciples of Jesus Christ. Then as disciples, we can truly put God first in our lives and He will reveal His plan relevant to every gift and talent He has given to us. We will be energized, motivated, and enthused. Then can we embrace the institution of the church that exist to enhance us and point the way to Jesus who has a plan for our lives.

Step 5: Know that all things work together for the good.

"We know that all things work together for good to those who love God, to those who are called according to His purpose" (Romans 8:28).

We must remember Jonah and how he wanted the people of Nineveh to be destroyed. However, it wasn't God's will or His purpose. God wanted the people to repent so He could bless them. They repented and God blessed them regardless of how Jonah felt. It's good to know that regardless of how many people may condemn you, God will forgive you if you just ask for forgiveness and turn from your ungodly ways. The Bible says that all things work together for them that love God, and Jesus said if you love God, you will keep His commandments. Therefore, love is an action word. If we love Him, we will keep His commandments and all things that happen in our life will work together for good. The reason it will work together for good is because God has a purpose and plan for everyone, as recorded in the Book of Genesis. No one exemplifies this principal like the steward Joseph. To summarize, Joseph was hated by his brothers who threw him into a pit to die. However, he was found and sold into slavery in another country and later falsely imprisoned. All of this happened so that he could be exalted in due time to be a ruler in Egypt at a time of famine. It was Joseph's faith, wisdom, and skill that sustained the people during the time of famine. It was God's will for Joseph to go from the pit to the palace through this gruesome process. It all worked together for good because of God's purpose.

Step 6: Know that you are more than a conqueror.

Romans 8:37 (AKJV) states, *"…in all these things we are more than conquerors through Him who loved us."* This means that as we follow God, we will be victorious in fulfilling God's purpose for our lives. Though we will not be exempt from trials and tribulations, we know that we will be victorious if we faint not. Even in death, we are conquerors. I Corinthians 15:54-55 (AKJV) reads, "…Death is swallowed up in victory. O death, where *is* thy sting? O grave, where *is* thy victory?" Therefore, we do not die but transition into eternal life with the Lord Jesus Christ.

Step 7: Know that God is on your side.

Psalms 56:9 (AKJV), states, "When I cry *unto thee*, then shall mine enemies turn back: this I know; for God *is* for me." Written by King David, Psalm 56 is encouraging because it teaches us that God hears our cries and answers us. David experienced God's deliverance multiple times. The king would humble himself and cry for help and God was faithful. In the Book of Jonah, it speaks twice about God hearing the cries of people. In Jonah 1:2, God stated that the wickedness of the people came up to him. We can interpret this as the people in distress and crying to the Lord God. After Jonah preached, God heard the cries of a repentant nation. God really does not want to destroy, but bless. He is consistent in loving and leading all people to His beautiful will for all mankind. After the people of Nineveh were led by their king to fast, pray, and turn from their wicked ways, God spared their lives. God is always on our side if we seek Him for direction.

REFLECTIONS

Review the Seven Steps of Deliverance. Which step or steps do you find the most challenging? Why?

REFLECTIONS

Which step towards deliverance are you now ready to concentrate on and apply? Why? What is your plan for applying the step?

CHAPTER 6

Understanding God's Love

Saved But Not Delivered: A Guide to Experience Joy and Peace

John 3:17 (AKJV)

For God did not send His Son into the world to condemn the world, but that the world through Him might be saved.

I truly don't believe that we understand how much God loves us. News Flash, God is not looking for people to punish! This was Jonah's issue with God and still is many people's issues with God today. While we should be looking forward for people to repent, some are looking for God to send judgment. John 3:17 explains that Jesus did not come to condemn the world but to save everyone. God's heart beats for souls. Therefore, our first thoughts, speech, and the preached word should be of His love and plans for mankind if we follow Christ Jesus. Only then should the Word be balanced with an understanding that we will reap what we sow.

In Luke chapter 10, a lawyer who was skilled in the Mosaic Law challenged Jesus. This lawyer knew the scriptures and asked Jesus two questions. First, he asked Jesus how could he inherit eternal life. Jesus asked him what was written in the law. The lawyer responded, "Thou shalt love the Lord thy God with all thy heart, and with all thy soul, and with all thy strength, and with all thy mind; and thy neighbor as thyself." Jesus told him to do this and live. But the lawyer wanted to justify himself and asked the second question, "Who is my neighbor?" At this point, Jesus decided to tell a parable about the Good Samaritan to further explain who is your neighbor and ultimately what is love. This story about the Good Samaritan is found in Luke 10:30-37.

> **30** *Jesus answered, "A man went down from Jerusalem to Jericho and fell among thieves, who stripped him of his clothing and wounded him and departed, leaving him half dead.*
>
> **31** *By chance a priest came down that way. And when he saw him, he passed by on the other side.*
>
> **32** *So likewise a Levite, when he came to that place, looked at him and passed by on the other side.*
>
> **33** *But a Samaritan, as he journeyed, came where he was. And when he saw him, he had compassion on him,*
>
> **34** *and went to him and bound up his wounds, pouring in oil and wine. Then he set him on his own donkey and brought him to an inn, and took care of him.*
>
> **35** *The next day when he departed, he took out two denarii and gave them to the innkeeper and said to him, 'Take care of him. I will repay you whatever else you spend when I return.'*
>
> **36** *"Now which of these three do you think was a neighbor to him who fell among the thieves?"*
>
> **37** *He said, "The one who showed mercy on him."*

Then Jesus said to him, *"Go and do likewise."*

Because Jesus knew the lawyer lacked the understanding of applying the Scriptures to everyday life, He spoke to him in a parable that served as a mirror. Jesus was not necessarily condemning the man, but shed light on the area of his life that was not committed to the things of God. This parable answered both questions. Jesus told the story of a man who had been robbed, stripped, beaten and left to die. Those who knew the scriptures, the priest and the Levite, passed him by. Instead, a Samaritan, who was considered beneath the Jews, helped the wounded man. Jesus' lesson to the lawyer taught that it is not enough to just know about God and quote the scriptures, but you must be God-like, showing the love of God by applying the scriptures to your life. Jesus used the parable as a mirror so that the lawyer could see his sin, make a change, and be converted. When we are like the priest and Levite who have not applied the word of God in our lives, we cannot perceive God's love and cannot do God's will which is to love.

God is a giver. We have to see that we were worthy of Jesus dying on the cross for our sins. If we can see the love that God has for us then we can see that person lying in the ditch over yonder and say, "Let's go get him!" How can we tell the Good News of Jesus Christ if we have not acknowledged His love, compassion, forgiveness, and mercy in our own lives? You can't give what you don't have. You can't give God's love to others if you have not received it for yourself. It affects your perceptions. Let's examine what God's Word says about love. In I Corinthians chapter 13 it states, "Love is kind and doth not behave itself unseemly." Walking by the wounded man is unseemly, just wrong. The Good Samaritan became emotional and with compassion went to him, cleaned his wounds, and placed him on a beast to transport him to an inn to take care of him. And it didn't stop there! He paid for someone to nurse him and promised to repay for additional costs when he returned. This act indicates love causes us to have compassion for one another and then to do something about it.

Throughout the Bible we read about Jesus's compassion, prior to performing a miracle. A compassionate person sees a person suffering and finds a way to alleviate their suffering. It is not empathy nor sympathy. Empathy means that you can identify with a person's grief and then share it with others for clarification. Sympathy means that you feel sorry for a person or situation and may gossip about it. However, only compassion causes a person to change the situation. If we are not motivated by the sufferings of people, then there is no ministry. Ministry rides on compassion.

The Bible states that Jesus performed many miracles because He was moved with compassion. Jesus was moved with compassion that motivated Him in Mark chapter 1 to heal the leper. He was moved with compassion and fed the multitude with the fishes and loaves. In Mark chapter 6, Jesus was moved with compassion and taught the people many lessons because they were like sheep without a shepherd.

If we are going to understand and apply God's love, then we must first accept the love that He has for us and then be moved with compassion to make a change for those who suffer physically or mentally. Because God was moved with compassion, He sent his Son Jesus the Christ to die on the cross for our sins and rise from the grave so that we may rise too and have life more abundantly.

REFLECTIONS

How do you know that God loves you? In what ways has He been compassionate towards you?

REFLECTIONS

In what ways can you show God's love and compassion for others?

Do you have a testimony of how you showed God's love and compassion? If so, please reflect and share.

Chapter 7

Press On...
Don't Look Back!

Saved But Not Delivered: A Guide to Experience Joy and Peace

Genesis 19:17

And it came to pass, when they had brought them forth abroad, that he said, Escape for thy life; look not behind thee, neither stay thou in all the plain; escape to the mountain, lest thou be consumed. (AKJV)

In Genesis chapter 19, God delivered Lot, the nephew of Abraham, from the cities of Sodom and Gomorrah. God had decided to destroy those cities because the outcry against its people had grown great in His presence. The sexual immorality of its residents was probably what influenced Lot's daughters to eventually commit incest with their drunken father. Lot was only delivered because his uncle, Abraham, interceded in prayer for him. He did not want to see Lot nor his family destroyed. In mercy, love, and grace, God sent two angels to rescue Lot and his family. However, to witness the promises of God, there was something they had to do.

The angel of the Lord gave specific instructions for Lot and his family's deliverance. These instructions can be used today as God is leading us out of any situation.

The first was, "Escape for your life." Destiny was waiting for them. Sodom and Gomorrah were not in their place of destiny.

The second instruction was, "Don't look back." In other words, don't long for the days of yesterday. Keep moving in the direction God leads.

The third instruction was, "Stay not in the plain." Leave it all. God had something better. Don't hang around the circumference of the situation. Move forward!

The last instruction was to "Escape to the mountain." God wanted to take them to higher ground.

The mountain symbolizes God's will, purposes, and plans for our lives. God is constantly trying to move us into what He created us to be. We were born equipped with the potential to be successful in the gifts and talents He has given us. Many of them are untapped. Therefore, God is constantly trying to bring out all the greatness He placed in us. As the Scripture reminds us, we were created in "His likeness." Therefore, when we accept Jesus Christ as Lord and Savior, we are born again. Our spirit connects with God's spirit and as we yield to the spirit of the Lord we experience God's transformational power!

Salvation and deliverance enables us to be who we were created to be - which is God's ultimate goal. However, we must yield to God's will. Such was the case of Jonah and the people of Nineveh. The people of Nineveh repented and God blessed them. This was not the case concerning Lot and his family. Lot's wife looked back and became a pillar of salt. Not following God's instructions for deliverance that He has provided will cost us our life and dreams. Not allowing God to transform us completely will cost us our peace.

Both Jonah and Lot had a relationship with God but resisted God's transformational power in their own lives. Even today, this is every Christian's challenge. Jonah did not have the love of God for mankind and Lot's life did not reflect God's standards. Had they both experienced God's transformational power in their lives, they would have experienced unspeakable joy. Jonah would have gone immediately to Nineveh to preach and rejoiced when they repented and served God. Lot and his family would have been a Godly example of a family reflecting God's standards. Both men were saved but not delivered! Even today, the choice is ours to be completely transformed by the power of God, or to remain ignorant and ineffective in areas that God wants us to be victorious. Deliverance is just as miraculous as salvation. It is the constant yielding to the Lord Jesus Christ.

The Bible says in 1Corinthian 2:9-10 (KJV) *"...that eye hath not seen nor ear heard neither have entered into the heart of man, the things which God hath prepared for them that love him. But God hath revealed the unto us by his Spirit: for the Spirit searcheth all things, yea, the deep things of God."* That's why we are encouraged to press on. *"I press toward the mark for the prize of the high calling of God in Christ Jesus"* (Philippians 3:14).

In Ephesians chapter 6:10-18, we learn how to press on. The Bible teaches us to be strong and to put on our armor so we can stand against the tactics and schemes of the devil. It states, *"Finally, my brethren, be strong in the Lord, and in the power of his might. Put on the whole armour of God that ye may be able to stand against the wiles of the devil. For we wrestle not against flesh and blood, but against principalities, against powers, against the rulers of the darkness of this world, against spiritual wickedness in high places. Wherefore take unto you the whole armour of God that ye may be able to withstand in the evil day, and having done all, to stand. Stand therefore, having your loins girt about with truth, and having on the breastplate of righteousness; and your feet shod with the preparation of the gospel of peace; above all, taking the shield of faith, wherewith ye shall be able to quench all the fiery darts of the wicked. And take the helmet of salvation, and the sword of the Spirit, which is the word of God: praying always with all prayer and supplication in the Spirit, and watching thereunto with all perseverance and supplication for all saints;" (AKJV).*

To press on, we can't look back. Jesus said in Luke 9:62 "…No man, having put his hand to the plough, and looking back, is fit for the kingdom of God" (AKJV). Neither can we stay in the plain and hang around the place that God is moving us away from in His plans. This reminds me of the wise men who followed the star to see the baby Jesus. They were warned in a dream to not go back to report to King Herod, therefore, they departed into their own country another way.

After Jesus has made a way, don't go back. We must move to higher ground and be what God intended us to be…effective and blessed. We must trust God with our future. Finally, we must put on the whole armor of God and not be ignorant of Satan's devices. As we move forward with God, we must remember to have faith and stand on the Word of God as Romans 8:31 (AKJV) says, "…*If God be for us, who can be against us?*"

REFLECTIONS

In what ways can you press on toward the mark of the high calling of God in your life?

What immediate steps can you take? What long-term goals can you set?

Saved But Not Delivered: A Guide to Experience Joy and Peace

REFLECTIONS

Paraphrase what it means to put on the whole armor of God.

Make it personal and meditate on what God is saying to you.

Ask, and it shall be given you;
seek, and ye shall find;
knock, and it shall be opened unto you:
(KJV)

RECOMMENDED READING LIST

- T.D. Jakes, *Women Thou Art Loosed!*

- Bishop I.V. Hilliard, *Daughters of Destiny, The Biblical Defense of Women's Rights*

- Myles Munroe, *In Pursuit of Purpose*

- Cynthia Heald, *Becoming A Woman of Excellence*

- Reverend Mrs. Charlotte S. Riley, Edited with an introduction by Crystal J. Lucky, *A Mysterious Life & Calling, From Slavery to Ministry in South Carolina*

- Gregory Dickow, *From The Inside Out, Fasting From Wrong Thinking*

- Jimmy Evans, *7 Secrets of Successful Families*

Reverend Wanda A. Allen

Reverend Wanda (Scruggs) Allen is serving as Pastor alongside of her father, Elder Walter W. Scruggs, who is Senior Pastor of Memorial Gospel Crusades Church in Philadelphia, Pennsylvania. Prior to Pastoring, she has served in various leadership capacities including youth, women and music ministries. In addition, she was Associate Minister at Vine Memorial Baptist Church in Philadelphia, Pennsylvania, under the Pastoral leadership of her father-in-law, Reverend Dr. James S. Allen.

Wanda Allen is a lifelong educator and has served as a public school teacher, administrator and an instructor on the university level. She holds a Bachelor of Arts degree from Cheyney University, Masters in Education degree from Temple University, Certificate in Distributed Leadership from University of Pennsylvania and a Certificate in Biblical Studies from Whetstone School of Biblical Studies. She has been the recipient of several educational and ministerial awards.

Wanda Scruggs Allen

Pastor Wanda is a highly respected and sought-out speaker who enjoys sharing the Gospel of Jesus Christ. She believes that salvation through Jesus Christ gives us the power to live victoriously and to overcome every obstacle. She enjoys sharing the love of Jesus Christ and preaching hope to all mankind. She continues to remind all of Jeremiah 29:11, "For I know the plans I have for you, declares the Lord, plans to prosper you and not to harm you, plans to give you hope and a future." Pastor Wanda lives with her husband, James S. Allen Jr., near Philadelphia, Pennsylvania, and they are both actively involved in ministry.

www.ingramcontent.com/pod-product-compliance
Lightning Source LLC
LaVergne TN
LVHW051511070426
835507LV00022B/3042